Biomes

Oceans

John Woodward

Chrysalis Education

BIOMES

DESERTS
GRASSLANDS
OCEANS
RAIN FORESTS
WETLANDS

Distributed in the United States by
Smart Apple Media
1980 Lookout Drive, North Mankato, Minnesota 56003

Copyright © Chrysalis Books PLC 2003

ISBN 1-59389-125-3

The Library of Congress control number 2003104995

Editor: Andrew Solway
Editorial Manager: Joyce Bentley
Designer: Mark Whitchurch
Consultant: Michael Allaby
Picture Researcher: Glass Onion Pictures

Printed in Hong Kong/China
10 9 8 7 6 5 4 3 2 1

Picture Acknowledgements
We wish to thank the following individuals and organizations for their help and
assistance, and for supplying material in their collections: Corbis 5 top (Robert Holmes),
10 (NASA), 37 (Roy Corral); Digital Vision *front cover*; Ecoscene 1 (Jeff Collett), 16 (Visual
and Written), 21 (Jeff Collett), 30 (Quentin Bates), 33 (John Corbett), 39 (Andrew D R
Brown); FLPA 32 (D Hall); NASA 7 (NOAA); Oxford Scientific Films 4 (Okapia), 12
(Daniel Valla/SAL), 13 (Waina Cheng), 15, 23, 31 (David Tipling), 42 (David Cayless);
Popperfoto 3 (Reuters), 18 (Reuters), 28, 29 (Reuters), 41 (Reuters), 44 (Reuters); Rex
Features 5 middle (Lehtikuva Oy); Science Photo Library 6 (Julian Baum and David
Angus), 8 (Peter Menzell), 14 (NASA/GSFC), 26 (Institute of Oceanographic
Sciences/NERC), 27 (Martin Bond); Still Pictures 5 bottom (Fred Bavendam), 17 (Mark
Carwardine), 19 (Norbert Wu), 20 (Norbert Wu), 22 (Sergio Hanquet), 24 (Hartmut
Schwarzbach), 25 (Jean Roche), 34 (David Drain), 35 (Pierre Gleizes), 36 (Andre
Maslennikov), 38 (Mark Edwards), 40 (Brecelj and Hodalic), 43 (Shehzad Noorani), 45
(Nigel Dickinson), 46 (Roland Seitre), 47 (Jeff Greenberg). Artwork by Michael Posen.
The pictures used in this book do not show the actual people named in the case studies
in the text.

CONTENTS

Hassan's Story

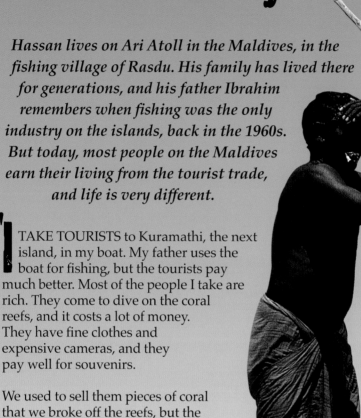

Hassan lives on Ari Atoll in the Maldives, in the fishing village of Rasdu. His family has lived there for generations, and his father Ibrahim remembers when fishing was the only industry on the islands, back in the 1960s. But today, most people on the Maldives earn their living from the tourist trade, and life is very different.

"I TAKE TOURISTS to Kuramathi, the next island, in my boat. My father uses the boat for fishing, but the tourists pay much better. Most of the people I take are rich. They come to dive on the coral reefs, and it costs a lot of money. They have fine clothes and expensive cameras, and they pay well for souvenirs.

We used to sell them pieces of coral that we broke off the reefs, but the government stopped us from doing that. Because the divers come to see the coral, we have to take care of it—and the fish that live on it. Down in south Ari

Atoll they used to mine the reefs for building stone, but the government stopped that, too. They're stopping everything that might harm the coral, including a lot of fishing. Many people say we have a right to fish where we like, but I don't agree. The fish are worth more to us in the ocean, attracting rich tourists.

In 1998, something terrible happened. The coral started dying all over the Maldives. The ocean was too warm, because of something called El Niño (see p. 13). The coral is growing again now, but they say it could happen again very soon because of global warming. If we have no coral, no one will come for the diving, and there will be no fish to catch. We will all be ruined.

But my neighbor says that global warming could destroy the Maldives altogether, because as the ocean warms up, the sea level will rise. It will flood the islands, because none of them are more than the height of a man above the waves. It seems impossible. Can he be right?"

Problems in other oceans

The Maldives is just one area where the ocean life is under threat from local and worldwide problems.

THE GALAPAGOS
Illegal fishing boats have been catching tuna in the Galápagos Marine Reserve, and killing dolphins in the process. All over the world, uncontrolled pirate fishing is threatening marine life.

THE BALTIC
The cold, enclosed waters of the Baltic are badly polluted by industrial chemicals, heavy metals, and pesticides flowing off the land in European rivers. Seals, sea eagles, and fish are all in serious trouble.

WESTERN AUSTRALIA
A planned resort for 2,000 tourists on the Ningaloo Reef may cause problems for the humpback whales, sea turtles, dugongs, and whale sharks that visit the reef each year, by increasing boat traffic and disturbance.

What Are Oceans?

Most of the world's surface is covered by deep oceans, which together make up by far the largest biome on the planet. Formed by the titanic geological forces that have shaped the continents, their waters conceal dramatic submarine landscapes of deep trenches, high mountains, and active volcanoes.

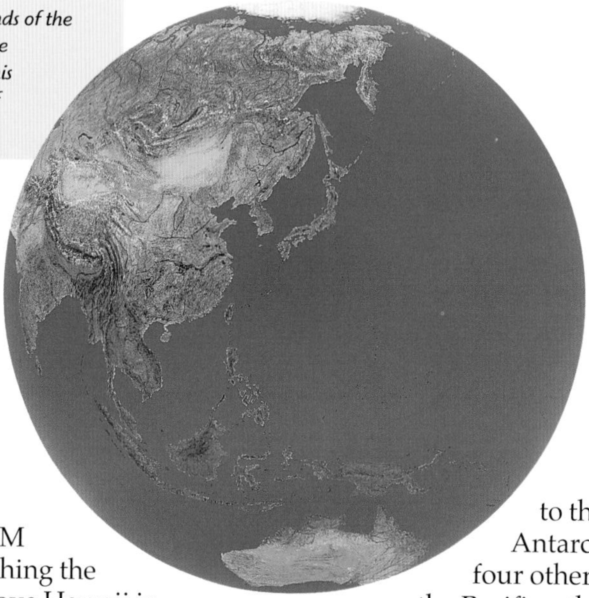

The continents and islands of the Earth are dwarfed by the vastness of its oceans. This picture shows just half of the Pacific Ocean.

A VISITOR FROM space approaching the Earth from above Hawaii in the Pacific Ocean would see a blue planet, because the Pacific covers almost half the world. It is bigger than all the continents put together—a vast expanse of water extending from Alaska to the fringes of Antarctica. There are four other oceans besides the Pacific—the Atlantic, the Arctic Ocean, the Indian Ocean, and the ice-bound Southern Ocean that surrounds Antarctica. Together, the oceans cover almost 70 percent of the Earth's surface.

What is a biome?

A biome is a major regional community of plants and animals, with similar life forms and environmental conditions. Each biome is named after its dominant feature, such as tropical rainforest, grassland, or coral reef.

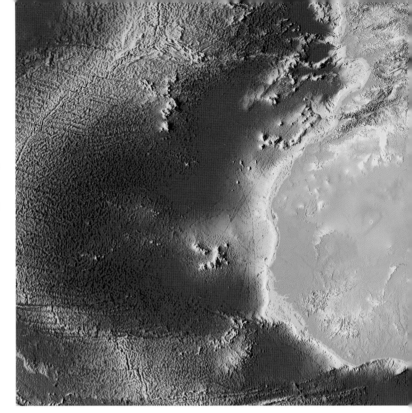

This photograph shows the ocean floor off the coasts of Spain and north Africa. In places, the rock of the ocean floor is split by deep rifts, or pushed up into long mountain ranges.

How deep are the oceans?

Oceans are not just broad puddles on the surface of the Earth. Their average depth is more than 2mi (3.5km), while the average height of the land above sea level is just 3,280ft (1,000m). In places, underwater trenches plunge to depths of 6mi (10km) or more; they could swallow Mount Everest with almost a mile to spare. The sheer volume of water in the world's oceans is enormous—it has been estimated at over 240 million cubic miles (a billion cubic km).

What's different about the ocean floor?

The ocean floor is made from a special kind of rock. It is very heavy and black, and quite different from the rock that forms continents. It is called basalt.

If you could cut the Earth in half, it would look a bit like the inside of a giant peach. On the outside is a thin crust, like the peach skin—except that the Earth's crust is not one continuous piece but is instead made up of several enormous pieces, called plates. Below the crust is a very thick layer of dense, heavy, hot rock called the mantle, which is like the flesh of a peach. At the center of the Earth is the "peach pit"—a core of metallic iron and nickel.

Basalt is formed from molten minerals that boil up from the mantle. The basalt of the ocean floor is lighter than mantle rock, so it lies on top of the mantle like a layer of oil on water.

The rock that forms continents is lighter than basalt, so the continents "float" higher in the mantle than the ocean floor. In some places, for instance along the fringes of the Atlantic, the ocean floor and the continental rock are locked together. But in other places, such as the Pacific coast of South America, the heavy ocean floor rock is being dragged beneath the lighter continental rock by movements within the Earth.

Molten basalt can erupt from oceanic volcanoes in spectacular "fire fountains." Mauna Loa in Hawaii (shown here) is a huge volcano that has grown up from the floor of the Pacific Ocean.

What makes the ocean floors move?

The core of the Earth is like a vast nuclear reactor. It generates huge amounts of heat, which makes the rock of the mantle extremely hot. The mantle rock is a lot hotter than the lava that pours from volcanoes, but it stays solid because it is under pressure from the huge weight of rock above it. This raises the melting point of the mantle rock and stops it from becoming liquid. Yet, despite this, it can flow sluggishly, like soft clay.

As heat rises from the Earth's core, it generates convection currents, just like the currents you see churning through a pan of boiling soup on the kitchen stove. And just as the soup boils up and around, so the mantle rock surges up toward the cool, hard crust of the Earth, spreads out, cools, and sinks again. It moves very slowly, at just an inch a year, but as it moves, it drags the ocean floors with it.

What causes ocean trenches and ridges?

In places where the mantle rock is cooling and sinking, it drags the ocean floor rock that rests on top of it down into the Earth. This creates deep ocean trenches like the 7mi (11km) Marianas Trench in the western Pacific. As the rocks grind their way downward, the friction causes volcanoes to erupt along the edges of the trenches. The volcanoes in Japan, Java, and the Andes mountains of South America were formed in this way.

As they are pulled down at the edges, the great plates of oceanic crust move apart to form immense rifts in mid-ocean. As these rifts open, the pressure on the hot rock below is released, so it melts. Molten rock squirts up into the cold ocean water and solidifies to form submarine mountain chains called mid-ocean ridges.

The longest of these, the Mid-Atlantic Ridge, is 43,500mi (70,000km) long, running from Spitzbergen in the Arctic almost to Antarctica. The two sides of the ridge are steadily moving apart, and this is pushing the Americas away from Europe and Africa. The same thing is happening to the Red Sea between North Africa and the Middle East, which is getting 1 inch wider every year. In a hundred million years' time, the Red Sea could be an ocean as big as the Atlantic.

As the old ocean floor is dragged down into the mantle at "subduction zones," the new ocean floor is created from molten basalt welling up and solidifying at mid-ocean ridges.

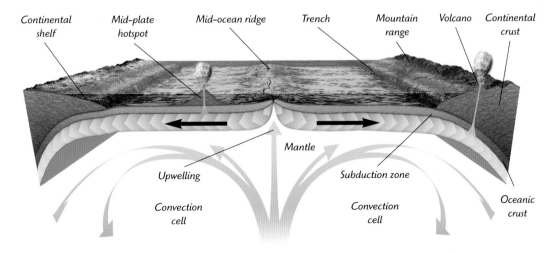

How Do Oceans Work?

The waters of the world's oceans are kept in constant motion by powerful currents that sweep across the globe. Driven by a combination of solar heat, the rotation of the Earth, and ocean winds, these currents have a huge influence on global weather systems and climate, for better or worse.

Heat from the Sun over a tropical ocean drives the swirling winds of a hurricane.

OCEAN WATER IS continually on the move. These movements are called ocean currents. They carry water around the ocean surface, and they also move it down into the depths, across the ocean floor, and up again. These surface and deep-water currents interact in a complex pattern.

The currents are driven by a combination of forces, including the temperature of the water. Close to the poles, the ocean water is extremely cold, and freezes at the surface. Since sea ice is pure water, the cold water beneath the ice becomes more salty and dense, and sinks to the bottom. In the north Atlantic this cold "bottom water" flows south toward the tropics, while at the surface, warmer water flows in from the Gulf of Mexico. The warm surface current is known as the Gulf Stream. It is the Gulf Stream that gives northern Europe its mild climate.

Ocean currents are also driven by the turning of the Earth. The rotation creates huge circular eddies (currents) at the surface. In the northern hemisphere, these currents move clockwise.

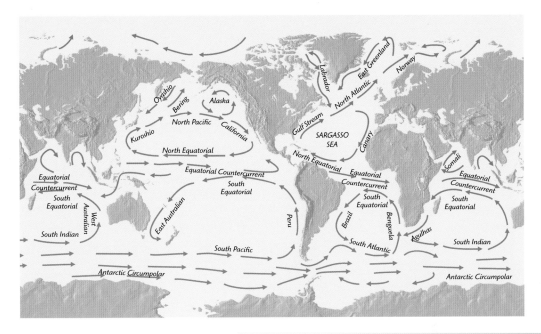

This map shows the major ocean currents of the world. The currents swirl around in great eddies, or "gyres."

They flow westward along the Equator, alongside similar currents that swirl counterclockwise in the southern hemisphere.

The movement of these huge masses of water from the tropics toward the poles and back again has a powerful effect on air temperatures above the oceans. Warm water carried toward the poles warms up the air above, making the climate milder. Warm air rises, and this causes "low pressure zones" that suck in air from areas where colder water is cooling the air and making it sink. The moving air masses create winds that blow across the oceans, and these then help drive the currents. So the winds and currents are intimately connected, and the world's weather is partly controlled by the movements of the oceans.

Where did all the water come from?

As the Earth was cooling down after its formation 4.6 billion years ago, huge clouds of volcanic gases poured from its interior. These included vast amounts of water vapor that eventually cooled and condensed to form the oceans.

The volcanic gases also included chlorine—the gas that gives public swimming pools their peculiar smell. The chlorine was dissolved in the early oceans, and it is possible that they smelled a bit like swimming pools. Over time, however, rivers pouring off the continents picked up other substances from the rocks and carried them into the oceans. These included sodium, a metal that reacts chemically with chlorine to produce sodium chloride, or salt. It is sodium chloride that gives ocean water its distinctive salty taste.

What causes waves and tides?

The wind also heaps up the waves that roll across the oceans. Waves are ripples on the ocean surface, like the ripples on the surface of a pond. Yet the weight of water in a wave can be colossal, and when it reaches the coast and breaks, toppling forward to crash on the shore, all that weight is turned into destructive power. Waves smash and grind at coastal rocks, breaking them slowly into tiny pieces, then sweeping away the pieces and piling them up as beaches and banks.

The Moon also affects the oceans. The Moon's gravity pulls on the water of the oceans as the Moon orbits the Earth. This causes the daily rise and fall of the tides. It also causes "tidal streams"—horizontal movements of water associated with the rise and fall of the tide. In places, these tidal effects can cause powerful local currents that can transform calm coastal waters into ferocious torrents and whirlpools, much more dangerous than the great waves of the open ocean.

Breaking waves pound at solid rock, splitting it into boulders and gradually reducing it to small stones and beach sand.

What is El Niño?

One of the most powerful ocean currents is the Humboldt Current, which sweeps up the western coast of South America, carrying cold water from Antarctica. At the Equator, it turns west past the Galápagos Islands and out into the Pacific Ocean. The cold waters of the Humboldt Current are rich in microscopic food, which supports much of the wildlife in the region. But each December, the current gets weaker as the strong winds that drive it ease off. This allows warmer water, very poor in food, to flow in from the north. This seasonal effect is called El Niño. It usually lasts for four to six weeks, but every few years, it can last for up to nine months, wiping out the food supply in the region. Fish vanish, seabirds starve, and the warm water disrupts the climate, causing droughts and coastal flooding throughout the tropics.

The disruption of the climate caused by El Niño can cause disastrous droughts in the drier parts of the world.

What Lives In The Oceans?

The oceans contain the biggest, most bloodthirsty killers on Earth, refined by evolution into marvels of speed and efficiency. But these spectacular hunters are just part of a huge and complex web of life that relies for its survival on clouds of microscopic floating plants and animals known as plankton.

ALL LAND ANIMALS depend on plants for their survival, and ocean animals are the same. Even the killer sharks that prowl tropical seas rely on plant life, because they prey on fish that have eaten smaller animals, which in turn have fed on plankton. This kind of feeding relationship is called a food chain—and in the ocean, all food chains lead to plankton.

Why is plankton important?

The microscopic green plants are the first and most important link in the chain, because they can turn raw chemicals into the proteins and

This "false color" satellite image shows amounts of plankton in the oceans. The pale green areas of the oceans have the most plankton—the darkest blue areas are "marine deserts" with no plankton.

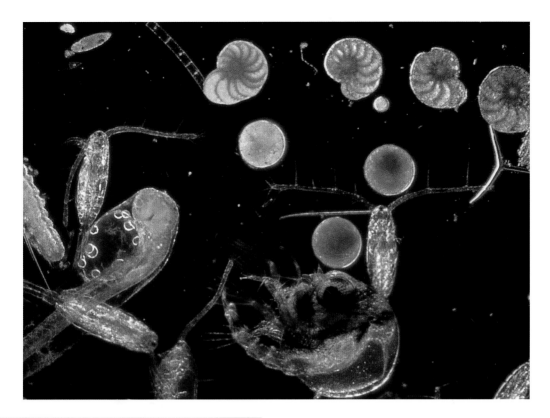

A magnified photograph of a sample of plankton. It shows a mixture of microscopic green plants and tiny animals, which all drift in the sunlit surface layers of the ocean.

carbohydrates that animals use as food. Tiny animals are part of the plankton too, feeding on the microscopic plants. Many of these animals are little bigger than the plants they eat. They include great swarms of shrimplike animals called krill, smaller creatures called copepods, and the tiny, floating larvae (young) of animals such as crabs, barnacles, mussels, clams, starfish, and sea urchins. All of these plankton animals are too small to swim against the ocean currents, and so they drift where the currents take them. Krill and copepods spend their whole lives adrift, while other planktonic animals only drift until they turn into adults.

What eats plankton?

In plankton-rich areas like the ocean
waters off western South America, the
plankton swarms attract schools of small
fish such as anchovies, sardines, and
herring. Many of them feed by straining
water through their gills to trap the
plankton. Bigger plankton eaters like the
enormous basking shark use exactly the
same method of feeding.

The even bigger baleen whales have their
own way of harvesting plankton. They
surge through swarms of plankton such
as krill, taking great gulps of water. Then
they use their tongues to push the water
out through the curtains of bristly baleen
that fringe their enormous mouths, and
the krill are trapped on the bristles.

The enormous mouths of these humpback whales
allow them to scoop up huge quantities of plankton.

What eats the plankton-feeders?

Schools of small plankton-feeding fish
such as herring are the main targets of
hunters like tuna, marlin, sailfish, small
sharks, and dolphins. Many of these are
built for speed, with massive muscles
and superb streamlining. A sailfish, for
example, can outswim a speedboat and
accelerate to speeds of 81mph (130kph)
or more as it closes in on its prey.

Sailfish hunt alone, but tuna and
dolphins hunt in packs. When they find a
school of food fish such as herring, they
surge at them in a group attack. The
herring defend themselves by forming a
tight, swirling ball of fast-swimming fish.
The hunters try to break up the ball, so
that they can pick off the fish one by one.
Dolphins use pulses of sound and bursts
of bubbles to confuse the school, and
often succeed in scattering and eating

them all. Tuna are almost as efficient, surrounding the school and diving in and out to snap up their victims in a feeding frenzy.

As the undersea hunters attack these swirling balls of fish from below, they often drive them toward the surface. Here, they may be targeted by ocean birds such as albatrosses, brown pelicans, gannets, and auks, which dive into the water to seize the fish in their bills.

The commotion of these attacks, and even the taste of blood in the water, can be sensed from far away. It alerts the most powerful predators of all—the orcas, or killer whales, and big sharks like the notorious great white and tiger sharks. These formidable killers target the tuna and dolphins rather than the schools of small fish.

Does anything live in mid-ocean?

Compared to the murky green waters often seen around coasts, the clear blue waters of mid-ocean look pure and unpolluted. Yet very little actually lives in these vast expanses of open ocean. They are like blue-water deserts.

One of the most famous is the Sargasso Sea. It lies in the middle of the North Atlantic, surrounded by a great swirl of ocean currents. These currents carry minerals that encourage plankton growth, but the minerals never reach the Sargasso Sea. As a result, there is no plankton and no fish, or very few. So the Sargasso Sea is literally the dead center of the ocean.

In South America, hungry orcas (killer whales) surge right out of the ocean to grab sea lion pups resting on the beach.

What survives in the black depths?

In the oceans, most of the action takes place within 660ft (200m) of the surface. Yet large areas of the world's oceans are almost two miles deep. What lives in this huge volume of ocean water?

The answer is not a lot, compared with the teeming life up near the surface. Below 660ft (200m), there is not enough light to support plants, so there is nothing to attract plankton-eating fish and their predators. But there is food. All the activity in the upper ocean creates a fallout of edible material, including dead plankton, scraps of meat, and even whole carcasses. It all sinks slowly into the black depths.

This "marine snow" of edible scraps is eaten by a variety of animals such as shrimp and jellyfish, which are preyed on in turn by deep-ocean fish and squid. Many of these glow in the dark, with a weird light produced by special cells called photophores.

Our knowledge of the deep oceans is put together from scraps of data gathered by submersibles like this "Deep Drone" surveyor.

The rows of blue light organs on the belly of the hatchet fish make it almost invisible from below when it is swimming in the deep ocean.

These deep-ocean killers often have huge mouths bristling with long, needlelike teeth. The teeth ensure that scarce prey do not escape, and their huge mouths, combined with stomachs that expand like balloons, mean that they can eat animals much bigger than themselves. These killers look terrifying, but most are surprisingly small. They simply cannot get enough food to grow any bigger.

Yet there are monsters in the depths. The colossal sperm whale routinely dives to 3,300ft (1,000m) or more, searching for its favorite prey, the giant squid. Squid can grow to 49ft (15m long), with eight arms and two long tentacles for catching fish. Giant squid have the biggest eyes in the whole animal kingdom. They are the size of dinner plates—up to 12in (30cm) across. These huge eyes enable the squid to see its victims in the dim blue twilight 2,600ft (800m) or so below the surface.

Why do some fish glow in the dark?

The hatchet fish lives in the deep ocean, where it is hunted by many bigger fish. Like many deep-water fish, it glows with an eerie blue light. Why?

Most fish that live in surface waters have silver bellies to match the silver glitter from the surface, making them almost invisible from below. In the depths, there is only a soft blue glow from above, so the hatchet fish generates a matching glow from rows of light-producing organs on its belly. This keeps the fish from appearing as a tempting black silhouette against the blue.

What Lives At The Ocean Edge?

The shallow fringes of the world's oceans are the richest of all marine habitats. The fertile, sunlit waters are often thick with plant life, and this supports a huge variety of animals. Many swim freely in the water, but many more stay anchored in one place for life, filtering their food from the water.

IN SOME PARTS of the world, such as volcanic islands, the deep ocean begins just offshore. But most continents have been so worn away at the fringes by the constant battering of the waves that their real edges are now underwater, several miles from the coast. The seabed slopes gently from the coast to this true continental edge, where it plunges into the depths. The region between the coast and the continental edge is called the continental shelf.

Thick "forests" of kelp (seaweed) off the Pacific coasts of North America swarm with food for animals such as these sea otters.

Filter-feeding animals like this tropical giant clam gather food by drawing plankton-rich water through their bodies and straining out the food.

What lives in the shallows?

Since they are surrounded by floating food, many continental shelf animals stay in one place and allow their meals to come to them. Mussels root themselves to rocks, and feed by sucking water through their bodies and filtering out the plankton. Sea anemones catch tiny animals using tentacles armed with stinging cells. Many marine worms live in tubes, and extend feathery fans to snare the floating plankton. And rocks, wrecks, even large seaweed are encrusted with colonies of sea squirts, sea mats, corals, and other plantlike animals, all living on the plankton in the water.

The waters of the continental shelves are among the richest habitats in the oceans. This is mainly because they are quite shallow. The seabed is rarely more than 590ft (180m) beneath the surface, so it lies within the zone of water that is lit up by the sun. Close inshore, the light allows seaweed to grow on the bottom, where it shelters all kinds of animals. The water itself is often thick with plankton, which thrives on the mineral nutrients swept in from the deep ocean and flowing into the sea from rivers. The drifting clouds of plankton feed a huge variety of other animals.

The stay-at-home animals are attacked and eaten by more mobile creatures such as starfish and sea urchins. Creatures such as crabs and sea snails are scavengers, living on scraps. Predators such as the octopus come out at dawn and dusk to hunt crabs and snails. Their excellent camouflage enables them to blend into their surroundings, and they grab passing prey with their long arms. Flatfish and rays cruise sandy areas searching for tubeworms and half-buried shellfish. They are then eaten by big fish such as conger eels and coastal sharks.

How do animals survive on tidal shores?

The richest coastal waters are often the shallowest, since these get the most light. But close inshore, the water drains away twice a day as the tide goes out. Few sea creatures can cope with this, but since there is so much food in the water, any animals that can survive exposure to the air can live there in huge numbers.

Rocky shores are encrusted with millions of barnacles, mussels, limpets, and other tough-shelled marine animals, which seal themselves up to sit out the few hours when the tide is out. Sandy shores may look empty, but the sand near the water line is full of buried shellfish, worms, sea urchins, and crabs, waiting for the tide to come back in again.

Some animals do not have to wait for the tide to come in. Shore crabs scurry about on the open shore searching for dead fish and other delicacies. They have gills for breathing in water, but on land, they survive by carrying their own supplies of water for breathing, just as scuba divers carry their own air supply in tanks on their back. Their tight shells protect them from drying out. On tropical shores, ghost crabs and fiddler crabs survive in a

Coral reefs are like underwater gardens, teeming with colorful life.

What are coral reefs?

Some of the most spectacular coastal habitats are coral reefs. They are created by corals, plantlike animals that are related to sea anemones. Corals live in colonies somewhat like flowering bushes: each "flower" is a separate coral, but they are all linked together. Reef-building corals make themselves tubes of chalky rock to live in, and over time, these rocky tubes build up to form a reef. Reefs are full of nooks and crannies that make ideal shelters from storms, tides, and enemies. Like the rainforests on land, coral reefs are simply bursting with life. They are home to thousands of different kinds of fish, shellfish, and other animals.

similar way. They swarm in the thousands on food-rich beaches.

Some of the best feeding grounds are the mudflats in sheltered bays and river estuaries. When the tide is out, many different kinds of birds probe the mud for worms and other creatures buried below the surface.

In the tropics, mudflats also support trees called mangroves, which grow from tangles of roots sprouting from the mud. Underwater plants called sea-grasses also colonize sheltered mudflats, and in warm seas, green turtles and strange seal-like manatees and dugongs graze on the sea-grasses.

Clamped tight to their rocks, limpets are able to resist drying out in the wind and sun at low tide.

How Do We Use The Oceans?

We use the world's oceans as highways, hunting grounds, and amusement parks. They are also rich sources of valuable fuels such as oil and gas. But as human populations grow and we use up resources on land, the oceans are coming under increasing pressure as we pollute them and overexploit their resources.

TWO-THIRDS OF the world's human population lives in coastal communities, because the oceans are rich sources of wealth. For centuries, oceans have provided a relatively easy way of transporting heavy loads and of trading with other countries. Many of the world's richest cities—places like New York, London, Tokyo, Hong Kong, Singapore, and Sydney—started life as seaports. Today, many of the city docks are almost deserted, but the cities they created are still flourishing.

The wealth of Hong Kong originally came from its harbor, which lies on one of the great marine trade routes of the world.

Simple, small-scale fishing is important to many coastal communities, and does little damage to fish stocks.

How do we exploit the oceans for food?

Much of the wealth carried on ships comes from other countries, but some is obtained from the oceans themselves. The most ancient of these ocean resources is food.

Fish and shellfish have been part of our diet for thousands of years. At first, people just gathered shellfish from the shores, but the development of primitive boats, nets, hooks, and lines soon enabled them to catch fish. This kind of small-scale fishing is still practiced in coastal communities all over the world.

About a century ago, fishing became more scientific as the development of steam fishing boats allowed large fleets to target schools of fish wherever they were. Throughout the 1900s, the fishing boats and their equipment became more efficient. Bigger and better engines meant that boats could follow the schools wherever they went.

One of the most important innovations has been the development of efficient onboard refrigeration systems, which allow the fish to be frozen as soon as they are caught. But frozen fish cannot be processed, so this then led to onboard fish processing, before the fish are loaded into the freezer. Fishing fleets with these facilities can stay at sea for weeks, and exploit fish stocks in remote oceans.

Fish and shellfish are still among the most important ocean resources. Vast quantities are caught for sale in supermarkets—fresh, frozen, and canned —and more are caught for processing into "fish meal," which is used for fertilizer and animal food.

The floors of some oceans are littered with manganese nodules. They are valuable sources of minerals, but mining them from the depths is difficult and expensive.

What else do we get from oceans?

More than a third of the world's salt comes from the oceans. It is an ancient industry, especially in warm countries, since salt can be extracted from seawater by simply flooding a shallow pool and letting the water dry out under the sun. The white crystals left behind are sea salt.

Ocean water contains many other minerals, including metals such as magnesium and even gold, but most of them exist in such small quantities that they are rarely worth the trouble of extracting.

Minerals under the seabed are another matter. About a third of the world's total reserves of oil and gas lie under the shallow seas of the continental shelves. These "fossil fuels" are so valuable— both as fuel and as the raw material for plastics—that huge sums of money have been invested in extracting them from beneath the waves. Roughly a quarter of the world's crude oil and about a fifth of the world's natural gas now come from offshore rigs.

The oceans can also provide other forms of power. Ocean winds, waves, and tides can all be harnessed to drive electricity generators, and these power sources could become very important in the future.

How do we enjoy oceans?

We all use power, and most of us eat fish, yet for most of us, the ocean means one thing—summer. Every year, millions of people head for the beach to enjoy the ocean. In many parts of the world, such as the Mediterranean, tourism is the main local industry. Hotels, restaurants, and marinas have spread along the shore, and the coastal shallows are full of swimmers, sailors, and scuba divers.

It all seems like harmless fun, but the huge numbers of tourists—and the facilities provided for them—can have a surprisingly big impact on ocean wildlife. Other activities can be even more damaging, causing pollution, extinction, and even the destruction of whole ocean habitats. We will look at these problems in the next few chapters.

Offshore wind farms provide electricity with no pollution, unlike burning fossil fuels. They help to reduce the problem of global warming.

DEBATE—Should we use the oceans to generate power?

- Yes. Fossil fuels such as oil are becoming harder to find, and they cause the air pollution that is leading to global warming. Power from ocean winds, tides, and waves will never run out, and does not cause pollution.
- No. The power plants usually have to be sited in places that are areas of natural beauty or important for wildlife. Interfering with the natural tidal flow is particularly destructive.

Are We Destroying The Ocean Wildlife?

In the past, people have destroyed whole populations of marine animals. The great whales that once roamed the oceans in the thousands have been almost wiped out, and many are now very rare. Overfishing of fish such as cod, herring, and tuna could easily destroy these animals, too.

Whaling using hand harpoons was difficult and dangerous, but the whalers still managed to destroy whole whale populations.

ON JANUARY 17, 1773 the ships *Adventure* and *Resolution*, commanded by Captain James Cook, became the first ships ever to cross the Antarctic Circle. Heading south on a voyage of exploration, they discovered an icy world teeming with life. The bleak, rocky islands were alive with seals and penguins, and the stormy waters of the Southern Ocean heaved with great whales. Greatest of all were the blue whales, up to 98ft (30m) long and weighing up to 150 tons—the biggest animals that have ever lived.

What happened to the whales?

By the late 1700s, seal and whale hunters in northern oceans were already running short of prey. Following Cook's lead, they headed south, and began one of the greatest mass slaughters in history. The fur seals were the first to suffer, clubbed to death for their pelts. A typical sealing ship might take up to 9,000 seals in just three weeks, and there were hundreds of such ships. By the 1830s, there were virtually no fur seals left, so the hunters switched to killing whales for their valuable oil.

Harpooning whales was a lot more difficult and dangerous than clubbing seals, but the invention of the explosive harpoon in 1864 enabled the whalers to kill virtually every whale they saw. By 1930, they were killing 30,000 blue whales a year. As the blue whales became scarce, they turned to right whales, humpbacks, and others. Before long, they were nearly all gone.

As whale populations dwindled, maximum catch numbers (quotas) were agreed to control the hunting. The quotas were set by the International Whaling Commission (IWC), which was set up for this purpose in 1946. But the quotas were often too high, and whale populations continued to fall. Eventually, pressure from the United Nations forced a total ban on commercial whaling in 1985. Although some countries still practice "scientific" whaling, whale numbers are gradually increasing.

In 1995, these Japanese whalers were still hunting whales in Antarctic waters, inside areas that are supposed to be internationally agreed whale sanctuaries.

Are fish being destroyed in the same way?

The story of whaling is the most dramatic example of ocean wildlife destruction, but some fish are suffering almost as badly. Fishing boats can now accurately locate schools of fish such as herring and tuna using electronic depth sounders or "fishfinders." They may then encircle the fish with a "purse seine" net that can be closed off at the bottom like a string bag, and scoop the entire school from the water. This technique virtually wiped out the herring stocks in the northeast Atlantic, and in 1976, herring fishing was banned in this region. Many tuna stocks have also fallen.

In contrast to such focused fishing, other fishing fleets use nets that catch virtually anything in their path. Trawl nets, for instance, are hauled across the seabed to catch fish such as hake, cod, and haddock. The trawls act like underwater bulldozers, killing and injuring many more animals than they catch. They also take so many fish that hake and cod populations in European waters are now at dangerously low levels. Quotas have been imposed, but as with the whaling quotas, the permitted catches are too high, so fish stocks are still declining. Unless something drastic is done, there may soon be no fish left in the northeast Atlantic.

In a single haul, this Icelandic purse seiner has netted an entire school of herring: around 300 tons of fish. Catches like these are destroying north Atlantic fish stocks.

DEBATE—Should fishing in some waters be limited?

- Yes. Some fish are now so rare that they may be wiped out altogether, which would destroy the fishing industries that depend on them.
- No. Thousands of workers in the fishing industry would lose their jobs, and whole coastal economies would suffer as a result.

Dumped on the dock in the snow, these porpoises were drowned in fishing nets set off the coast of Norway.

Are other marine animals suffering, too?

Fish are the main food of many marine animals, so if the fish disappear, these animals have nothing to eat. Seabirds such as puffins depend upon small fish such as sand eels and capelin to feed their young. But these fish have become profitable to catch, and the fishing fleets scoop so many from the north Atlantic that several breeding colonies of puffins have vanished altogether. Seabirds can also become tangled in fishing nets and drown.

During the 1980s, huge drift nets several miles long were developed to catch tuna and squid in the Pacific. Known as "wall of death" nets, these snared any ocean animals that ran into them, including diving seabirds, seals, dolphins, and turtles. One fishing trip by a fleet of 32 Japanese drift-netting boats resulted in the death of over 1,000 small whales, 52 seals, 22 turtles, and over 50,000 sharks. Such death rates led to these kinds of nets being banned in 1993, although enforcing the ban has not been easy.

Another method of fishing involves attaching up to 20,000 baited hooks to a line up to 75mi (120km) long, and trailing it through the water. Since the drift-net ban, this "longlining" technique has become popular with tuna boats. Unfortunately, longlining doesn't just catch tuna. Seabirds try to snatch the bait from the line before it sinks, and inevitably, some are hooked in the bill or throat and drown.

Fish markets like this one in Thailand could become a thing of the past if fish stocks are wiped out by overfishing.

What is being done?

The most notorious accidental victims of fishing are dolphins. They often hunt in partnership with tuna, and the tuna fleets discovered that encircling a dolphin school with a purse seine net was a sure way of netting a school of tuna. But the dolphins were netted, too, and drowned. When this became widely known, there was a public outcry, and the tuna fleets were forced to use divers and opening panels in the nets to release the dolphins before they became fatally entangled. Tuna caught in this way—or by using poles and lines instead of nets—is labelled "dolphin friendly."

Yet the problem has not gone away. Many of the early "dolphin friendly" tuna nets still snared a lot of dolphins, and recent designs are not much better. In early 2002, fishing nets equipped with metal grids intended to divert dolphins and sea lions were being tested in New Zealand. The testers discovered that the animals were ramming the grids and suffering concussions before escaping, and then drowned as a result. But at least the problem is being looked at. The days are gone when it was acceptable to accidentally catch dolphins along with other fish.

How can seabirds be protected?

There are ways of preventing the accidental capture of seabirds by longlining boats. Some of the main victims of longlining capture are albatrosses. These magnificent birds spend most of their lives in the air, soaring over the Southern Ocean. But they often follow ships, including

Many seabirds like this gannet are snared in discarded fishing nets when they dive to catch fish. Unable to get back to the surface, they drown—and their tattered bodies end up as food for beach scavengers.

longlining fishing boats, and since they feed on fish and squid, they are easily attracted to baited lines, and are hooked and dragged under. Setting the hooks at night, weighting the lines, and using bird scarers all help stop accidental bird capture. These measures are now enforced by law, and as a result, the legitimate longliners have reduced their total seabird catch by an amazing 90 percent. But many longline boats operating in the Southern Ocean are illegal, and these "pirates" still kill up to 100,000 seabirds each year, including around 20,000 albatrosses.

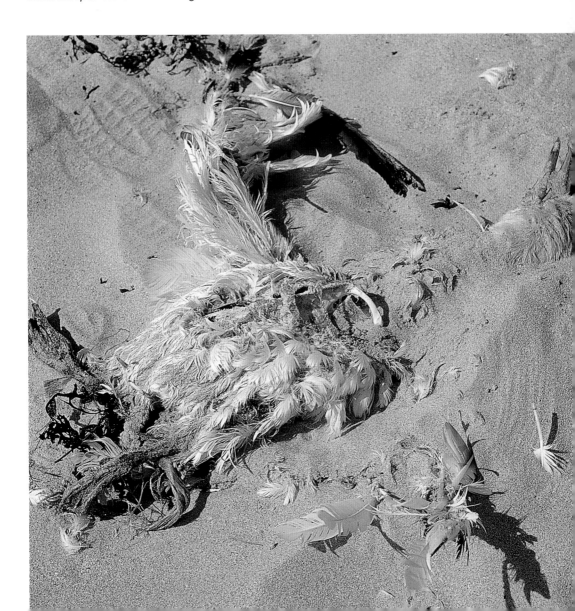

Are We Poisoning The Water?

Every year, vast quantities of waste are deliberately or accidentally dumped in the oceans. This waste includes dangerous chemicals, oil, and sewage, as well as huge amounts of garbage. The pollution threatens to poison the water of oceans and shallow seas, destroying their wildlife.

IN EARLY 2002, a routine check on marine life in the Severn estuary in western Britain discovered that the fish were radioactive. Their bodies contained tritium, which is a product of nuclear power plants. These plants pump millions of gallons of tritium-contaminated waste water into the ocean every year, in the belief that it will disperse and then disappear.

But the tritium levels found in the fish show otherwise. The Severn estuary is not the only example of this—there are thousands of others around the world. Slowly but surely, we are poisoning the oceans.

All over the world, coastal industries like this magnesium plant in northern England discharge toxic effluent into the sea.

Offshore dumping is often targeted by environmental protest groups. Here, French Greenpeace activists try to prevent the dumping of toxic sludge.

How does pollution get in the water?

For centuries, we have used the oceans as dumping grounds for our garbage. Pipelines from coastal towns carry raw sewage and waste from factories out beyond the tide line and into the water. Garbage is routinely thrown overboard from ships. For years, oil tankers have cleaned out their tanks at sea, flushing waste oil into the oceans. Bales of domestic waste, drums of toxic (poisonous) chemical waste, and even sealed containers of nuclear waste are taken out to sea and dumped. Much of this activity is illegal, but it happens anyway because dumping from ships is difficult to stop.

This deliberate pollution of the oceans is just part of the problem. Huge quantities of fertilizers, pesticides, and other agricultural chemicals drain off the land, into rivers, and out to sea. Silt and sludge from mines and quarries also end up in the ocean. As much as 40 percent of all ocean pollution comes from the land in this way. Meanwhile, offshore drilling for oil pollutes the water with oil-contaminated mud, and every day, fishing boats lose nets that drift in the ocean for years, trapping and killing marine wildlife.

In 1978, the oil tanker *Amoco Cadiz* lost its steering and ran aground on the rocky coast of Brittany in northwest France. The hull was ripped open, spilling 223,000 tons of crude oil over 93mi (150km) of coastline. The following year, a "blow-out" on the oilrig *Ixtoc 1* in the Gulf of Mexico gushed 475,000 tons of crude oil into the sea. More recently, in 2002, the damaged oil tanker *Prestige* spilled about 5,000 tons of oil onto the Spanish coast before sinking with over 70,000 tons of oil still on board.

Oil floats on water, causing great oil slicks that drift with the winds and currents. They can be broken up with detergents somewhat like dishwashing liquid, but this just makes a toxic sludge that sinks to the seabed. If the oil slick blows onshore, it smothers and poisons the coast, and in remote areas with rich wildlife, the effects can be catastrophic.

Which sea areas are most vulnerable?

The effects of pollution are worst in small seas, since the pollutants are not washed away into the vastness of the ocean. The North Sea, for example, is badly polluted with oil from drilling platforms, industrial waste, and pesticides, and the Baltic Sea is even worse. The poisons in the water affect fish, seabirds, and seals, making them prone to disease. In 1988, nearly 18,000 harbor seals died from a bacterial disease, almost certainly because their natural defences were damaged by poisoning.

In the Mediterranean, one of the main threats to wildlife is pollution by raw sewage. At least 80 percent of the 500 million tons of sewage dumped in the Mediterranean every year is untreated. Besides the disease risk, this also works a bit like throwing fertilizer into the sea. It makes the plankton grow much faster than usual, causing "blooms" of microscopic plants. Some of the planktonic plants that grow in sewage-polluted waters can release poisons that kill fish and other animals, and when the plankton bloom dies, it creates a foul, decaying sludge that uses up all the oxygen in the water.

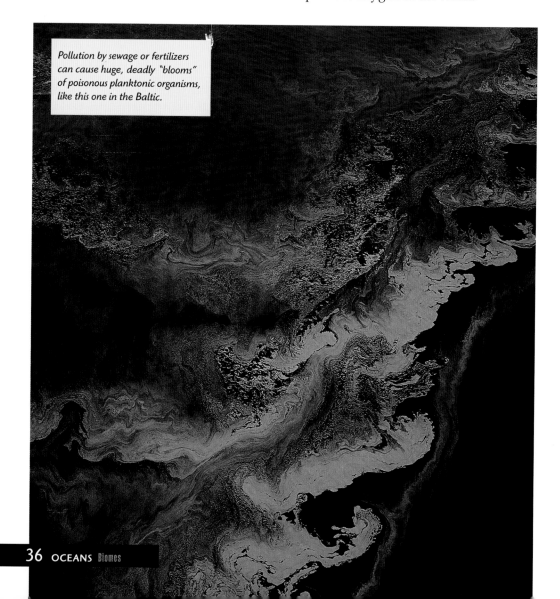

Pollution by sewage or fertilizers can cause huge, deadly "blooms" of poisonous planktonic organisms, like this one in the Baltic.

What can be done?

There are laws against deliberately polluting the oceans. They may be hard to enforce, but they are having some effect. The amount of oil pollution from shipping, for example, has gone down since the 1970s. Many accidents can be prevented through improved technology. Problems such as raw sewage are harder to deal with, because many coastal communities cannot pay for proper sewage processing.

After the accident the Exxon Valdez *was refloated and repaired. This picture shows the tanker after it was refloated.*

Black death

In 1989, the tanker *Exxon Valdez* spewed 35,000 tons of oil into Prince William Sound, Alaska, after the captain mistook his route and ran the ship onto rocks. Although it was small by some standards, the oil spill polluted an area that was teeming with wildlife. Up to 300,000 seabirds and about 5,500 sea otters died, as well as millions of smaller animals. It was the most damaging oil spill in history. The sea otters are still suffering liver damage, years after the disaster, because of toxic oil in their diet.

What Is Happening Along The Coasts?

In the summer, everyone heads for the coast to enjoy the beach and the water. But the hotels and other developments that are built to cater for tourists—and earn money for local people—are turning wild coastlines into coastal towns. They are also threatening to destroy the marine wildlife that many of the tourists come to see.

THE POWER OF the ocean is most obvious on the world's coasts. Great waves crash into cliffs, grinding them away through erosion and carrying off the pieces to build beaches from shingle and sand. The spectacular coastal landscapes created by these processes attract millions of tourists.

Yet the tourists that visit coasts are destroying many of the most fragile coastal habitats. The money to be made from tourism encourages the construction of hotels all along the shore, and these have to be protected by sea walls. The natural shoreline is sealed beneath concrete, and the whole system of erosion and beach building is upset.

Meanwhile, much of the plant life along the shore is stripped away. This may include salt marshes and tropical mangrove swamps, both rich habitats for marine animals. When plant life along the shore is stripped away, bare soil is washed into the ocean.

The crowds of tourists that descend on the beaches of the Mediterranean each summer are causing a massive sewage pollution problem.

Natural coastal landscapes like this scene in Cornwall, western England, are easily destroyed by insensitive developments designed to attract tourists.

Marine reserves

Some coastal waters have been declared "marine reserves." All fishing is outlawed, along with any other damaging activity. But enforcing the law is not easy. The waters around Cocos Island off Costa Rica, for example, have been declared a fully protected World Heritage Site. Yet every night, they are invaded by illegal shark fishing boats. These lay longlines up to 30mi (50km) long, which catch thousands of sharks each month, as well as turtles, dolphins, and swordfish. There are not enough rangers to police the reserves properly, and the rich marine life of the island may be destroyed.

What are the main problems?

Coral reefs are particularly vulnerable to the washing of soil from land into the ocean, because corals need clear, sunlit water to survive. Large areas of coral have been destroyed like this in the Caribbean. Sea-grass beds—vital food sources for manatees and dugongs— can be smothered in the same way. They may also be scoured away by changes in the flow of the tides, or destroyed by dredging for building sand.

Other victims of coastal development include sea turtles, which emerge from the sea to bury their eggs on deserted beaches. Each species (kind) of turtle uses the same beaches each year. Kemp's Ridley turtle, one of the rarest, uses just a few sites on a 12-mi (20-km) stretch of beach in Mexico. Conservation organizations such as WWF have had some success in protecting Kemp's Ridley turtle, but if the nesting beaches of this or other turtle species are destroyed, the turtles will probably disappear completely.

Is tourism itself causing problems?

Unfortunately, yes. Thousands of visitors to coastal resorts may spend their time sailing, waterskiing, fishing, or scuba diving. These activities may seem harmless, but they mean trouble for coastal wildlife. Boat propellers injure marine mammals such as dolphins, manatees, and seals. Sea angling and spear fishing can threaten rare fish. The collection of reef specimens by scuba divers has damaged many coral reefs, and boat anchors often tear up big chunks of coral.

At the end of each day, the tourists want to eat local food. At many beach resorts this means fish, and the demand may be met by drastic methods. On the reefs off the Philippines, fish are caught illegally by tossing dynamite into the water. The explosion kills or injures every animal within range—not just the edible fish—and shatters the coral. Reef fish are also caught for exhibition in local aquariums, using cyanide (a deadly poison) to stun the fish in the water—a technique that kills far more than it catches. Raw sewage from coastal resorts is often dumped in the sea, and this adds to the destruction.

A solitary mangrove clump is all that survives of a tropical mangrove forest on the coast of New Guinea, swept away to make room for coastal development.

They may be beautiful, but coral reef fish in public aquariums are often caught by releasing poison into the sea to stun them.

Can tourism be a good thing?

Some tourists help preserve natural coastal environments. This is because they are willing to pay higher prices than normal to stay on coasts that do not have buildings like high-rise hotels, and are still rich in wildlife. The extra amount of money that these "ecotourists" pay means that local people can make a good living without overdeveloping the coastline. This approach has been adopted on the Australian Great Barrier Reef, which is the world's largest coral reef system. Yet even here, the sheer number of visitors threatens the reefs.

DEBATE—Is fish farming a good use of coastal resources?

- Yes. Breeding fish such as salmon in submerged cages eases the pressure on wild fish, provides employment in remote coastal regions, and produces plentiful protein-rich food.
- No. The water can become contaminated with fish food, fish excrement, antibiotics given to the fish to prevent infections, and the parasites that infest farmed fish.

How Is Climate Change Affecting The Oceans?

The world's climate is always changing. Slow, natural cycles bring worldwide heatwaves and ice ages that last thousands or millions of years. But over the last century human activity has caused a rapid warm-up that could have dramatic effects on the oceans and on the people who live near them.

THE WORLD'S CLIMATE has always changed very slowly, but now it is changing much faster. The change may not seem fast by human standards: in Alaska, average temperatures have risen by almost 2°F per decade over the past 30 years. But this is a lot faster than any natural cycle of climate change. And as far as scientists can tell, the root cause is pollution of the atmosphere.

The glass roof of a greenhouse allows light energy through but stops heat energy from escaping. Greenhouse gases in the atmosphere work in the same way.

The atmosphere doesn't just provide the air we breathe. It also protects us from the most dangerous of the Sun's rays and acts something like the glass of a greenhouse, letting light in by day but keeping heat in at night. The "glass" is really a mixture of gases, including carbon dioxide, which are particularly good at keeping the heat in. So the more "greenhouse gas" that there is in the atmosphere, the warmer the Earth gets.

Scientists analyzing air bubbles preserved in ancient polar ice have discovered that the amount of carbon dioxide in the atmosphere has risen steadily over the past 150 years. The increase almost exactly matches the rise in global temperature. So it seems that rising carbon dioxide levels are the main cause of global warming. Most of the extra carbon dioxide is being released by burning carbon-rich fossil fuels such as coal, oil, gasoline, and natural gas. These are used in electricity generating stations, car engines, and home heating. So the more power we use, the worse it gets.

DEBATE—Should we cut greenhouse gas emissions?

- Yes. The 1997 Kyoto Protocol calls upon each nation to cut its emissions of carbon dioxide and other greenhouse gases by about 7%. This would slow down global warming and climate change.
- No. The US government argues that cutting its emissions by 7% would make little difference to global warming, but would mean drastic cutbacks in industry, putting many Americans out of work.

As global temperatures rise, so do sea levels, causing regular flooding in low-lying regions such as Bangladesh. Eventually, such countries could disappear completely beneath the waves.

What will happen to the ocean water?

When water heats up, it expands to take up more space. So as the world gets warmer, sea levels rise. They have already risen by 4–8in (10–20cm) since 1900, and are predicted to rise by up to 35in (88cm) by the year 2100. Flooding will become routine, and many coastal communities could be swept away.

Things could get even worse. Immense volumes of water are locked up in the ice sheets that cover Greenland and Antarctica. If these start to melt—and a global temperature rise of only 7°F might be enough—the consequences could be catastrophic. Ice acts like a mirror, reflecting light back into space, so if there is less ice, the planet will absorb more light and more heat. Eventually, there could be a runaway thaw, and all the meltwater would cascade into the oceans.

If the ice caps melted, it would cause a sea-level rise of up to 164ft (50m). Coral islands like the Maldives would disappear, low-lying countries such as Bangladesh would become shallow seas, and major coastal cities throughout the world would be swamped. Since two-thirds of the world's population lives in coastal communities, most of us would be flooded out.

The polar bear is becoming a casualty of global warming, because its sea ice habitat is melting beneath its feet.

Catastrophic storms like the hurricane that devastated this Central American town could become more frequent as the climate changes.

What else could happen?

The warm Gulf Stream that gives Europe its mild climate is powered by ice forming on the fringes of the Arctic Ocean. This makes the salty water flowing north colder and even saltier, so it sinks and flows south along the ocean floor. As it sinks, it draws warm surface water north to take its place. But satellite and submarine measurements have found that the ice in the western Arctic is 40 percent thinner than it was 30 years ago. If ocean temperatures rise to the point where surface ice stops forming altogether, the water beneath it may stop sinking. This would stop the "pump" that powers the Gulf Stream

(see p. 10), and Europe could become as cold as Labrador in eastern Canada. Tropical currents are being affected right now. El Niño, which affects the weather in the eastern Pacific, is caused when warmer water pushes cold currents to the south (see p. 13). El Niño events are happening more often, and there is evidence that this is linked to global warming. If so, we can expect serious El Niño events every year, along with all the storms, floods, and droughts that they cause in the tropics. The rest of the world will suffer the fallout from these extreme weather patterns, and our weather could become even less predictable than it is now.

What Lies Ahead?

The oceans are huge, but they are not limitless. We are discovering this the hard way, as fish become scarce and marine habitats such as coral reefs are damaged. But if we act responsibly, we can help the oceans recover to full health, and maybe give ourselves a more secure future.

MUCH OF THE ocean floor has never been explored, and probably never will be. It is an alien world, more mysterious than the surface of the Moon. The vastness and mystery of the oceans has encouraged us to treat them as if they had no limits. For centuries, we have fished them for food, and put nothing back except our garbage. And up to a point, the oceans can cope. Surviving fish eventually breed and produce more fish. Garbage such as sewage and oil eventually breaks down and becomes harmless. It is even possible that the plankton in the oceans may multiply to absorb much of the extra carbon dioxide that we are pumping into the atmosphere.

But meanwhile, things are going wrong. Many fish are becoming scarce. Pollution is damaging coastlines. Ocean currents and weather systems are changing as global temperatures rise, causing more storms, flooding, and droughts. Rising sea temperatures are killing the world's coral reefs. It looks bad, and it could get worse.

Every seashell bought by a tourist encourages local fishermen to ransack the ocean for anything that might earn a few dollars.

Manhattan may seem a long way from the Maldives, but the pollution released by all these cars helps cause the global warming that is killing the world's coral reefs.

What can we do?

We can do a lot. We can eat a wider variety of fish, and fewer of the species that are getting scarce. We can reject tuna caught using methods that harm dolphins and other ocean life. When we visit the coast, we can avoid activities that damage marine habitats such as coral reefs, and stop buying souvenirs made from coral, seashells, and turtle shell.

Yet the main reason why the oceans have gotten into this state is that there are too many people using too much energy and dumping too much garbage. A typical American, for example, uses three times more materials and energy than the global average, and the US produces more than a third of the world's carbon dioxide. If we all threw less away, turned down the thermostat or air conditioning and made fewer car trips, it would have a big impact on pollution and global warming. It might make all the difference for the future of the oceans.

REFERENCE

OCEAN FACTS

- The total ocean area is 139 million sq mi (361 million sq km): 70% of the world's surface.

- The Pacific Ocean is 10,560mi (17,000km) wide, and contains 50% of the world's water.

- The oceans represent 80% of the living space on Earth.

- About 80% of the ocean is more than 1mi (3km) deep.

- The deep ocean floor covers about 116 million sq mi (300 million sq km), of which just 4 sq mi (10 sq km) have been explored.

- Mid-ocean ridges are the largest geological structures on Earth.

- Ocean temperatures range from 86°F (30°C) to around 30°F (−2°C) (the freezing point of salt water).

OCEAN DEPTHS

- The photic zone (where light can reach) is from 0 to 660ft (0 to 200m).

- The twilight zone is from 660 to 3,300ft (200 to 1,000m).

- The continental shelves are between 390ft and 1,300ft (120m and 400m) deep.

- On average, the ocean floor is 12,240ft (3,730m) deep.

- Oceanic trenches can be up to almost 7mi (11km) deep (the Marianas Trench in the western Pacific).

ICE

- Antarctic sea ice covers between 1.5 million (summer) and 8.5 million (winter) square miles of ocean.

- Arctic sea ice covers between 2.5 million (summer) and 5.4 million (winter) square miles of ocean.

- The Antarctic ice cap contains 7.2 million cubic miles of fresh water (70% of the world total).

- The Greenland ice cap contains 600,000 cubic miles of fresh water.

OCEAN DYNAMICS

- A typical big storm wave may be 49ft (15m) high.

- The largest recorded wave was 111ft (34m) high and traveled at 63mph (102kph).

- A typical ocean current moves at 6mi (10km) per day.

- A fast current moves at 56–99mi (90–160km) per day (Gulf Stream, north Atlantic).

- The biggest tidal range is 49ft (15m) (Bay of Fundy, Nova Scotia, eastern Canada).

Ocean Life

- The largest sea animal is the blue whale. It can be 108ft (33m) long and weigh 150 tons.

- The longest sea animal is a siphonophore (an animal related to jellyfish) that grows to 130ft (40m).

- The largest fish is the whale shark, which can be 46ft (14m) long.

- The fastest swimmer in the ocean is the sailfish, which can swim at 80mph (130 kph).

- The weight of krill in the Southern Ocean is estimated at up to 500 million tons.

- 80% of the plankton in the oceans consists of small, shrimplike animals called copepods.

- 90% of the world's fish live in coastal waters, and there is 1,000 times more life in the ocean shallows than on the deep ocean floor.

- The richest coral reefs are home to more than 700 species of coral, 5,000 species of mollusks, and 2,000 species of fish.

- The Great Barrier Reef off eastern Australia extends for 1,240mi (2,000km), covers 77,200 sq mi (200,000 sq km), and is visible from the Moon.

Ocean Uses

- 65% of cities with populations of more than 2.5 million are on coasts. Several are at sea level, or even below.

- The world's busiest port, Rotterdam in the Netherlands, handles 250 million tons of cargo every year. Nearly half of this is oil and gasoline.

- 10% of the fish caught worldwide are taken by traditional fishing methods. Commercial fishing fleets take the other 90%.

- 75% of fish caught commercially are used for food; 25% are used to produce fish oil and fertilizer.

- Fish and shellfish provide 5–10% of the world's food supply, and 10–20% of the world's protein.

- Fish and shellfish farming accounts for around 4% of total food production from the sea.

- 150 million tons of oil are extracted each year from the bed of the North Sea alone. In 1990, there were 149 oil drilling platforms in operation.

- The tidal power plant in the Bay of Fundy, Nova Scotia, eastern Canada, produces up to 20 megawatts of electrical power, or 1% of the electrical needs of Nova Scotia.

Wildlife Threats

- Ninety million tons of fish are caught worldwide every year.

- Between 90 and 95% of the world's fish stocks are already being exploited at their maximum levels.

- In the Mediterranean, the estimated maximum sustainable yield of fish is less than 1.4 million tons. The actual weight of fish caught is nearly 2 million tons.

- About 2 million tons of tuna are caught worldwide every year.

- In 1986, 133,000 dolphins were killed by purse seine tuna fishing in the eastern Pacific alone. Today, fewer than 2,500 dolphins are killed in this way each year.

- An estimated 35% of the northern right whales that die in the North Atlantic are drowned when they become entangled in fishing nets.

Water Pollution and Coastal Problems

- Over 40% of marine pollution has its source on land.

- In 1983, a "bloom" of toxic marine algae, caused by pollution, contaminated shellfish in the western Philippines, causing 278 cases of paralytic shellfish poisoning.

- During the 1950s, consumption of seafood contaminated by mercury pollution led to more than 900 cases of mercury poisoning around Minemata Bay in Japan. About 100 of these cases were fatal.

- The *Exxon Valdez* oil spill of 1989 polluted 100 sq mi (260 sq km) of Alaskan sea and shore with about 11 million gallons of crude oil.

- Coastal communities produce about 700 million tons of solid sewage per year.

- In the Santos estuary in Brazil, 118 cubic yards (90 cubic meters) of sewage are poured into the water every second.

- Up to 70% of the world's coral reefs are dead or dying.

- In a single Malaysian state (Sabah), 40% of the coastal mangrove forests have been destroyed—an area of over 460 sq mi (1,200 sq km).

CLIMATE CHANGE

- The combustion of coal, oil, and natural gas accounts for roughly 80% of all carbon dioxide emissions.

- Carbon dioxide in the atmosphere has increased by 25% over the last century.

- Without emissions-control policies, atmospheric concentrations of carbon dioxide are expected to rise from today's 367 parts per million (ppm) to 490–1260 ppm by the year 2100. This would represent an increase of between 75% and 350% since 1750.

- Climate models predict that the global temperature will rise by about 2.5–10°F by the year 2100.

- The global average sea level has risen by 4 to 8in (10 to 20cm) over the past 100 years. It is expected to rise by another 3.5–35in (9–88cm) by 2100.

- Sea ice in the Arctic Ocean has thinned by 40% in the past three decades, and its extent has shrunk by 10–15%.

GLOSSARY

atmosphere The blanket of gas that envelops the Earth. It is mostly nitrogen and oxygen, with small amounts of carbon dioxide and other gases.

basalt A heavy, dark rock that forms the floors of the oceans, and some oceanic islands such as the Galápagos, Hawaii and Iceland.

climate The weather pattern in a particular area, including seasonal changes.

continent A slab of relatively light rock that "floats" on the heavier rock of the Earth's mantle. The Earth has seven continents: Africa, Antarctica, Asia, Australia/Oceania, Europe, North America, and South America.

continental shelf The submerged fringe of a continent, covered with sea water to a depth of less than 1,300ft (400m).

coral reef A ridge of limestone rock built up from the stony "skeletons" of anemonelike sea creatures called corals.

current A large-scale movement of ocean water caused by heating and cooling combined with the rotation of the Earth.

drift net A fishing net that hangs in the water like a curtain, from floats at the surface.

El Niño A change in the Pacific Ocean currents near the Equator, which forces warm water further south than usual. This affects marine wildlife, and causes changes in weather patterns.

erosion The grinding away of rocks by natural forces such as ocean waves.

fossil fuels Carbon-rich substances such as coal, oil, and natural gas, formed from ancient plants and animals. The energy absorbed by the plants and animals in life is "fossilized," and released when the fuel is burned.

global warming A rise in global temperatures caused by polluting gases in the atmosphere, which trap heat like a blanket. This is known as the greenhouse effect.

greenhouse gas One of the gases that is polluting the atmosphere and causing the warming of the Earth (the greenhouse effect). One of the main greenhouse gases is carbon dioxide.

habitat The natural home of a particular living thing, or group of living things.

heavy metals Poisonous metals such as lead, zinc, copper, and mercury that are often released in industrial waste.

longline A very long fishing line with thousands of baited hooks attached to it, used to catch fish such as tuna.

mangrove A kind of tree that grows in coastal mudflats, forming forests or mangrove swamps.

mantle The thick layer of heavy rock that lies beneath the Earth's crust, and forms most of the volume of the Earth.

mid-ocean ridge A double chain of underwater mountains that extends along a rift in the ocean floor. New ocean floor is created at mid-ocean ridges, as the Earth's crust on each side is pulled apart.

minerals The natural materials that make up rocks. They are carried in ocean water, and many are used as nutrients by the tiny plants of the plankton.

nutrients Any substances used by living things to build their bodies or turn into energy, but especially the minerals used by plants and oceanic plankton.

ocean floor The bed of the deep ocean, beyond the continental shelves. It is made of basalt covered with fine silt, or "ooze."

pesticides Poisonous chemicals used to kill weeds and insect pests, which drain into rivers and into the oceans.

photophore A light-producing organ, found on many deep-sea animals.

plankton The living things, mostly microscopic, that drift in the ocean. Includes tiny plants called phytoplankton, which can make food using the energy of the Sun, and floating animals called zooplankton.

pollution Anything that spills into the air or water, and is not part of its natural chemistry. Includes both poisons and nutrient-rich fertilizers and sewage.

purse seine A fishing net that is set to encircle a school of fish and then closed off like a purse, so no fish can escape.

quota A maximum number of fish (or other animals) that can be caught during a particular period.

salt marsh A grassy swamp that develops on sheltered, salty mudflats in cool climates; the nontropical equivalent of a mangrove swamp.

scuba diver A human diver using an oxygen tank and breathing apparatus. The word "scuba" is made up of the initial letters of Self-Contained Underwater Breathing Apparatus.

sea-grass A flowering plant that grows in shallow sea water, resembling grass.

tide A movement of water from one place to another caused by the gravity of the Moon, and modified by the gravity of the Sun. Makes the water level rise and fall, and causes local water flows called tidal streams.

trawl A sock-shaped fishing net dragged across the seabed to catch fish that live on the bottom, such as flatfish and cod.

trench A deep rift in the ocean floor, created when oceanic crust is dragged down into the mantle rock by movements within the Earth.

upwelling An upward movement of mineral nutrients from the ocean floor caused by ocean currents, creating extra-fertile zones that support a rich variety of marine life.

FURTHER INFORMATION

BOOKS

Blue Planet by Alistair Fothergill (BBC, 2002)
A beautifully illustrated survey of ocean habitats and wildlife. Accompanies a series of videos from the BBC series of the same name.

Whales and Dolphins by Dr. Anthony R. Martin, (Salamander Books, 1990)
A comprehensive guide to all the world's whales and dolphins.

Atlas of the Oceans edited by Dr. D. L. Elder and Dr. J. C. Pernetta (Chancellor Press, 1991)
Maps of all the oceans, showing key habitats and the effects of industry and pollution, accompanied by superbly illustrated sections explaining the natural habitats and the threats they face.

The Living Planet by David Attenborough (BBC, 1984)
A classic text covering the world's biomes, with an excellent section on the oceans.

Sealife: A Complete Guide to the Marine Environment edited by Geoffrey Waller (Pica Press, 1996)
A good introduction to the complex sciences of oceanography and marine biology, containing information that is hard to find elsewhere.

The Encyclopaedia of Underwater Life edited by Dr. Keith Banister and Dr Andrew Campbell (Unwin, 1985)
A superb reference to almost every kind of animal that lives in water, from sharks to microscopic invertebrates. It is particularly informative on the biology of strange and obscure marine organisms.

The Atlas of the Environment by Colin Tudge (Helm, 1988)
A well-illustrated book covering the ecology of the planet and the effects of human activities, with useful sections on the oceans.

Great Waters by Deborah Cramer (Norton, 2002)
An account of an Atlantic voyage, with discussion of overfishing, global warming, pollution, and other important marine issues.

The Fatal Impact by Alan Moorhead (Penguin, 1968)
An account of the invasion of the South Pacific in the 1700–1800s, following the voyages of Captain Cook. Describes the destruction of the wildlife and the native cultures of the South Sea Islands, New Zealand, and Australia.

Great Barrier Reef by David Doubilet (National Geographic, 2002)
Exquisite photography of the world's greatest coral reef, with informative text.

The World Atlas of Coral Reefs by Mark D. Spalding, Corinna Ravilious, and Edmund P. Green (University of California Press, 2001)
A survey of the coral reefs of the world, with maps and photographs, highlighting the threats to their future.

Poles Apart by Dr. Jim Flegg (Pelham, 1990)
A highly illustrated introduction to the wildlife that lives in and around the icebound oceans of the Arctic and Antarctica, and the human impact on the polar regions.

Sharks by Michael Bright (Natural History Museum, 2002)
A guide to some of the most powerful predators in the ocean, including all the latest research findings.

MAGAZINES

National Geographic
A monthly magazine covering new discoveries about animals, plants and habitats, with extensive coverage of conservation issues – many involving the oceans.

ORGANIZATIONS

WWF-USA
1250 24th Street N.W.
P.O. Box 97180
Washington, D.C. 20090-7180
www.worldwildlife.org

Friends of the Earth
1025 Vermont Avenue, N.W.
Suite 300
Washington, D.C. 20005
www.foe.org

Greenpeace
702 H Street N.W.
Suite 300
Washington, D.C. 20001
www.greenpeaceusa.org

The Cousteau Society
870 Greenbrier Circle
Suite 402
Chesapeake, VA 23320
www.cousteausociety.org

WEBSITES

www.divediscover.whoi.edu
An interactive tour of mid-ocean ridges and underwater volcanoes, with pictures and videos shot from deep-water submersibles.

oceanexplorer.noaa.gov/
Follow ocean explorations, learn about ocean exploration technologies, and look at marine plants and animals on the website of the National Oceanic and Atmospheric Administration.

www.bbc.co.uk/nature/ programmes/tv/blueplanet/
The website of the BBC's excellent series about ocean life, with features, quizzes, and information.

INDEX